SNEAKY
SALAMANDERS

by Suzanne Paul Dell'Oro
with Andrés Varela-Paul

photographs by John Netherton

Lerner Publications Company • Minneapolis

Text copyright © 1999 by Lerner Publications Company
Photographs copyright © 1999 by John Netherton,
except as noted.

Additional photographs reproduced with permission:
© Rob and Ann Simpson, p. 12; © Nature's Images, pp. 13,
19 (both); © Dwight Kuhn, p. 15; © David Liebman, p. 26.

Website address: www.lernerbooks.com

Curriculum Development Director: Nancy M. Campbell

Words in *italic type* are explained in a glossary
on page 30.

Library of Congress Cataloging-in-Publication Data

Dell'Oro, Suzanne Paul.
    Sneaky salamanders / by Suzanne Paul Dell'Oro
with Andrés Varela-Paul ; photographs by John
Netherton.
        p. cm. — (Pull ahead books)
    Includes index.
    Summary: Introduces the physical characteristics,
behavior, habitat, and life cycle of salamanders.
    ISBN 0-8225-3612-9 (hardcover : alk. paper). —
    ISBN 0-8225-3618-8 (pbk. : alk. paper)
    1. Salamanders—Juvenile literature. [1.
Salamanders.] I. Varela-Paul, Andrés. II. Netherton,
John, ill. III. Title. IV. Series.
QL668.C2D45   1999
597.8'5—dc21   98-5198

Manufactured in the United States of America
1 2 3 4 5 6 — JR — 04 03 02 01 00 99

Salamanders are good at hiding.

Where is the sneaky salamander
in this picture?

This is a salamander.

Most salamanders are no longer
than your hand.

Salamanders see poorly. They run slowly. They have no claws.

Salamanders must be sneaky to keep from being eaten.

A salamander is a kind of
animal called an *amphibian.*

Most
amphibians
live part of
their lives
in water
and part
on land.

Like all amphibians,
salamanders are *ectotherms.*

When the air or water is cold,
their bodies become cold.

Salamanders must keep
their skin wet.

Salamanders breathe and drink
through their wet, slimy skin.

Slimy skin helps them
escape enemies.

How can slimy skin help
salamanders escape this raccoon?

Slimy skin makes salamanders
slippery and hard to catch.

Some salamanders have poison
in their skin.

Poison salamanders
are brightly colored.

Salamander tails break off
if they are grabbed.

The salamander runs away.
Soon it will grow a new tail.

Some salamanders can grow back other missing body parts, too.

Even legs and eyes grow back!

Salamanders are *carnivores.*

Carnivores hunt and eat other animals, like this baby frog.

ZAP! This salamander
has caught a worm.

How do salamanders find
the animals they eat?

Salamanders use their strong *sense of smell* to hunt.

When they catch an animal, they swallow it whole.

They even eat the eggs
of other salamanders!

Salamander eggs are soft and clear.

What can you see inside these eggs?

When most babies *hatch*, they do not look like their parents.

What is different?

Most baby salamanders
hatch underwater.

These babies are called *larvae.*

They have tiny, weak legs
and wide tails.

Larvae swim like fish.
They breathe like fish, too.

Larvae have feathery *gills* behind their eyes.

Gills gather tiny air bubbles from water for breathing.

Some larvae grow into adults underwater.

Others change so they can leave the water.

These larvae grow stronger legs
for walking on land.

Some larvae also grow *lungs*
for breathing air.

Some baby salamanders
hatch on land.

These babies have strong legs
from the start.

As salamanders grow,
their skin gets tight.

New skin grows, and
the old skin peels off.

No matter how big
a salamander grows,

it still must be sneaky to stay alive.

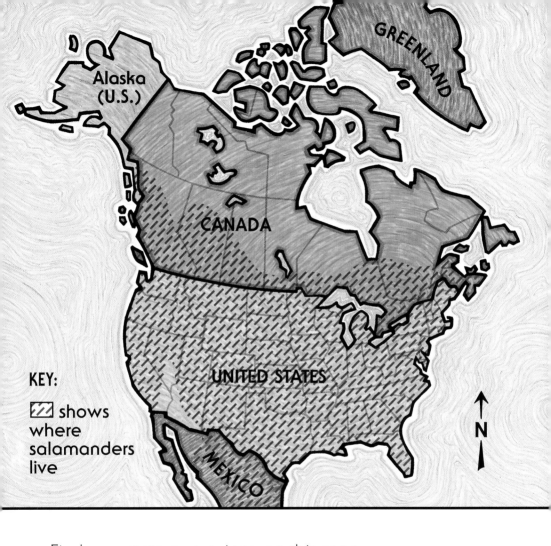

KEY:

shows where salamanders live

Alaska (U.S.)

GREENLAND

CANADA

UNITED STATES

MEXICO

N

Find your state or province on this map.
Do salamanders live near you?

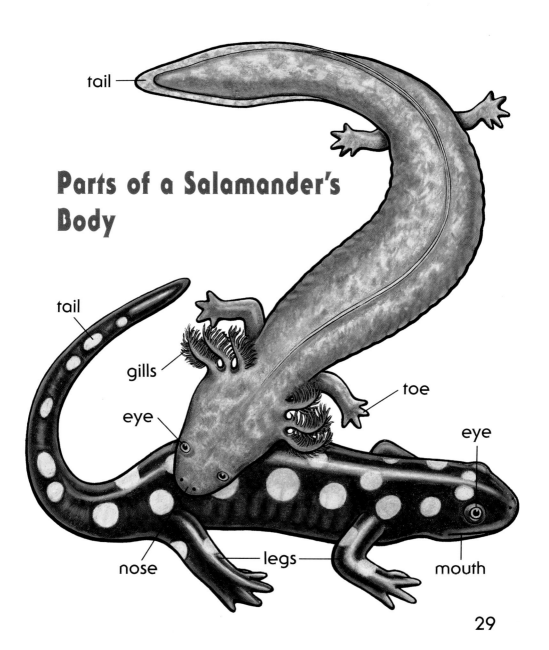

Parts of a Salamander's Body

tail

tail

gills

eye

toe

eye

nose

legs

mouth

29

Glossary

amphibian: an animal that has slimy skin and usually spends part of its life in water and part on land. (Frogs, toads, and salamanders are amphibians.)

carnivores: animals that eat other animals

ectotherms: animals whose body heat changes to match the warmth or cold around them

gills: outer body parts that gather tiny air bubbles for breathing underwater

hatch: to come out of an egg

larvae: baby salamanders that live in water

lungs: inner body parts that help some animals breathe out of the water

sense of smell: one of the five ways animals get information about things around them. (The other senses are seeing, hearing, touching, and tasting.)

Hunt and Find

- salamanders **eating** on pages 14–15, 17, 31
- a salamander **enemy** on page 9
- salamander **larvae** on pages 19–22
- a salamander with **peeling skin** on page 26
- **salamanders in water** on pages 13–14, 17, 19–23, 31
- **salamanders on land** on pages 3–5, 7–8, 10–12, 15–16, 19, 24–27

The publisher wishes to extend special thanks to our **series consultant,** Sharyn Fenwick. An elementary science-math specialist, Mrs. Fenwick was the recipient of the National Science Teachers Association 1991 Distinguished Teaching Award. In 1992, representing the state of Minnesota at the elementary level, she received the Presidential Award for Excellence in Math and Science Teaching.

Hugo Dell'Oro

About the Authors

Suzanne Paul Dell'Oro lives in Minneapolis, Minnesota, with her husband, three children, and the family cat. She writes about many different things. She wrote about salamanders with the help of her young son Andrés, who likes to study animals that have sneaky tricks. Suzanne and Andrés have seen many salamanders, but never in the wild—salamanders are too sneaky!

Brenda Campbell

About the Photographer

John Netherton has been a nature photographer for more than 30 years. He has taught and traveled throughout the United States and in many other countries. His work has been published in hundreds of books and magazines. Through these he shares his respect for nature and his commitment to recording it carefully. John has provided photos for four books in Lerner's Pull Ahead series. He lives in Nashville, Tennessee, and is the father of three sons: Jason, Joshua, and Erich.